my heart is hitchhiking down peachtree street

by J. Fergus Evans

Co-produced by Contact and supported by the Albany

First performance at Contact: 27 February 2012

The Artists:

Solo Performer & Writer:

J. Fergus Evans is a yarn-spinnin', boy-kissin' spoken word and performance artist. He is a founding member of the award-winning Atlanta-based performance collective Twinhead Theatre. Fergus's work focuses on restaging spoken word using video, soundscaping and sculpture.

www.jfergusevans.com

Creative Mentor:

Laura Mugridge is a theatre maker, improviser and stand-up comedian. Laura is the creator of Fringe First Award-winning solo show *Running On Air* and is currently developing new piece *The Watery Journey of Nereus Pike* as well as caravan-based pop-up performance events 'The Campsite'.

www.lauramugridge.co.uk

Set Designer:

Kat Heath is the resident designer for Theatre Delicatessen and has designed for The Old Vic Tunnels, The Southbank Centre, Soho Theatre and Latitude Festival. She has worked with dreamthinkspeak, Geraldine Pilgrim, and Punchdrunk, and received two Best Set Design nominations at the 2011 Off West-End Awards.

www.i-m.co/katheath/Katheath/

Animator:

Laura Richardson is a Manchester-based illustrator. She has worked as a concept artist for various independent film companies, as well as BBC Yorkshire. She also illustrates for publications and has hosted a number of solo exhibitions.

www.rolaricho.tumblr.com/

Video and Lighting Designer:

Andrew Crofts is a lighting designer and technician who regularly works with Imitating the Dog, Proto-type Theater and Contact. He is a founding member of the pervasive gaming company Larkin' About.

www.larkinabout.net

Dramaturge:

Jackie Hagan is an accomplished performance poet, stand-up comedian and arts facilitator. Awarded Best Emerging Poet 2006 by The Poetry Kit, she has had two poetry collections published (Citizen32 2005, Flapjack Press 2010).

www.flapjackpress.co.uk

Tour Manager:

Jack Dale is a technician and lighting designer who works with Reckless Sleepers, Proto-type Theater and Plane Performance. He is also the Production Manager for Flare International Theatre Festival.

www.jack-dale.co.uk

Producer:

Jenny Gaskell is an independent producer who works with Live at LICA, The Future, touring performance *The oh f*ck moment* and is the creator and producer of ACE funded Manchester citywide festival 'Lost & Found'.

www.the-future.co.uk

J. Fergus Evans

my heart is hitchhiking
down peachtree street

OBERON BOOKS
LONDON

WWW.OBERONBOOKS.COM

First published in 2013 by Oberon Books Ltd
521 Caledonian Road, London N7 9RH
Tel: +44 (0) 20 7607 3637 / Fax: +44 (0) 20 7607 3629
e-mail: info@oberonbooks.com
www.oberonbooks.com

A catalogue record for this book is available from the British
Library.

PB ISBN: 978-1-78319-005-8
E ISBN: 978-1-78319-504-6

Cover design by Roshana Rubin-Mayhew

Book illustrations by Laura Richardson

Printed and bound by Marston Book Services Limited, Didcot.

Visit www.oberonbooks.com to read more about all our books
and to buy them. You will also find features, author interviews and
news of any author events, and you can sign up for e-newsletters
so that you're always first to hear about our new releases.

Characters

FERGUS

You are led down a hallway, in a building you thought you knew but you're pretty sure you've never been down this hallway. It's hard to tell, because it looks like any other hallway in the building, and the door you're asked to stand in front of looks like any other door. You knock softly.

FERGUS: Come in.

You open the door. Inside is a small room filled with objects – old battered suitcases are stacked up in corners, rusty lanterns swing from the ceiling. A taxidermied alligator peaks out from a corner and paper cicadas swarm along the walls, in between framed pictures of black bears and peaches. The air is warm and sticky. There is a drawing of a statuesque drag queen weeping, and a winking alligator. Next to a fireplace sits a man (FERGUS) in a dirty baseball cap. A warm smile splits his bushy beard. Behind him, gingham curtains frame a window, which contains an animation of a tree, leaves rustling.

FERGUS: Come in, take a seat. Get comfortable. So… welcome to Georgia. Have you ever been to Georgia? So I know this isn't actually Georgia, but it's as close as I could get. I like it. Oh! Before we go any further, just a couple of quick health and safety things. There's a lot of stuff in here, so please just be careful. Also, the copperhead snake is one of the most poisonous snakes in the world, and it's indigenous to Georgia. Its bite is unlikely to kill you, as anti-venom is readily available at most hospitals. However, its venom deteriorates human flesh quite quickly, so its bite is likely to leave a lasting scar. One of the cool things about the copperhead is that its first bite is a dry bite, so it's like a warning. I mean, it's still going to hurt, but at least you won't get a scar. Another cool thing about the copperhead

snake is that it rarely strikes above the ankle, so as long
as you're wearing a good sturdy pair of hiking boots you
should be fine. In Georgia, we always wear our hiking
boots when we're out in the woods, or doing our grocery
shopping, or getting into bed. Can I just check your shoes
really quickly?

You show him your shoes. FERGUS looks dubious.

FERGUS: Okay, well if at any point you feel any sudden
pinches around your ankle, can you just let me know?

Anyway, so let's get to know each other a bit more.
What's your name?

You tell him your name.

FERGUS: And *(Insert your name here.)*, where would you call
home?

You tell FERGUS the name of the place you consider to be home.

FERGUS: And is that where you live now? Is it where you
were born? Do your parents live there? Your children?

Copperhead

(*Agkistrodon contortrix*)

One of the reasons I made this show is because I'm really
interested in people's definition of home – and how it
changes over time. I just think it's really interesting that

Sometimes home sits heavy in your bones
so as you know you'll never leave

Sometimes home opens up, all elastic
tissue and sinew, swallows whole all
the places you've been, or missed –

For me, mostly, home is wishing I was in Atlanta in August

heavy with heat

drunk with magnolia dreaming I
try to hold my home in my hand but it's as viscous as humidity
as solid as a heatwave…

My heart is hitchhiking on Euclid Avenue
(even as I speak to you)
Sweaty feet stuffed into sneakers
a thumb and fist thrust out like an invitation
(even as I speak to you)
My heart is hitchhiking

trying to find his way to you
hoping you'll be happy when you see him. He'll
lay his backpack down
unpack stories of hope and longing
and he'll be long gone come morning
(My heart isn't very good at staying)

In Atlanta, I saw days so sticky with summer you could
shower for hours
and still smell the heat on you hands, the scent stuck in the
creases of your fingers.

In Atlanta, I saw the asphalt crack, then turn liquid –
magmous – black tar rivers and
the cicadas are singing

My heart is hitchhiking down Peachtree Street
(even as I speak to you)
Each car that passes is a possibility.
(even as I speak to you)
My heart is hitchhiking down Peachtree Street

My heart is sharing half a Camel Light with a black drag
queen called Crow.
She's got a smile she's got to screw on tight at each corner
and mean black eyes like a snapperhead
But my heart, he's singing her love songs.
He can't help it.
He's crooning country roads

and lonesome winds whistling through pine trees, he
sings her
sweetheart songs
(sock-hop and promise songs)
songs about forever –
and they both know it's only gonna last as long as this half
a cigarette
but
my heart, he's a charmer...

This one summer day I watched this train go by and
(I was stuck at this crossing, so)
It was summer
and the sun smelled like
soap and
growing, the kind of
sunshine that sticks in your throat –
So
One day I watched this train go by
(I was stuck at this crossing)
just watched the red light flashing
And the noise of train like a fist hit me
deep, the noise was like water, rushing like a river, like the
Mississippi, rushing itself to an oceanic ending.
One day I watched a train go by
and thought about leaving –

*Behind FERGUS, a rough wind rustles the animated tree, and the
last remaining leaves spin to the ground.*

FERGUS: So just a couple of other things you should know for your own safety, that to be honest you'd probably already know if you'd grown up in Georgia.

1. If you ever happen to cross paths with a black bear, it's really important to play dead. See, black bears aren't carrion eaters, so if they think you're already dead they'll just leave you alone. So if you see one, just drop to the ground and go limp. And I know it's scary, but even if it comes up to investigate and sort of nudges you with its paws, if you want to survive – play dead. Even if it starts to rip open your insides, and nuzzle its muzzle towards your kidneys, play dead. And even if it gets your head in its jaws and sort of starts crunching your skull, well, you know.

2. Your mother loves you, no matter what.

3. If you're ever being chased by an alligator, you need to remember that they're surprisingly fast on dry land. Really fast. But the thing is, their legs are really short and stumpy, which means they can't change direction very quickly. So if you're ever being chased by an alligator on dry land, you just need to run in a zigzag pattern, and you should survive.

So there's this park about three miles from my high school.

It's called WP Jones. I don't know who he was or why he was so important that we had to commemorate him with a park. I'm sure I could probably Google it, but I don't know. It just never felt that important.

In fact, I'm not actually sure that the park itself was that important. I'm not even sure why I'm telling you about it. It's a pretty standard park – there's a playground, and a covered area for when it rains. There's a BBQ pit, and picnic tables. There's a stationary old-timey caboose, which is sort of a weird thing to have in a park – I think it was there so little kids can play in it, and learn about trains and stuff. But mostly bored teenagers would hang out in there to smoke weed.

Also, for a while I was convinced that this park was an ancient woodland filled with nature spirits. This may be closely related to the smoking in the caboose tradition.

As FERGUS speaks, a thick mist descends and obscures the tree in the window. When it clears, it's night time. The tree is bathed in the light of the full moon, and stars twinkle in the pitch sky.

Have you guys ever seen *King of the Hill*? Well, there's this episode...actually, I'm suddenly realising that *King of the Hill* pretty accurately summarises what it's like growing up in the South. I mean, that's Texas and this is Georgia, but if you squint your eyes it's pretty much an accurate account of my life. I'm Bobby Hill. I'm a thirty-one-year-old Bobby Hill and I'm sorry you paid good money to come see this show when you guys probably could have all pooled your money together and bought a *King of the Hill* box set. Sorry about that. Anyways, there's this episode of *King of the Hill* where Bobby falls in with the wrong crowd and decides he wants to become a warlock. Have you seen that one? It's brilliant.

And again, creepily true to life. When I was fourteen (Jesus, I can't believe I'm telling you this) I became a Wiccan. I wore pewter dragon pendants around my neck and doodled green men onto the tops of my Converse. I cast a love spell on a boy named Ben. It didn't work. It did, however, require stealing my mother's opal earrings. Though upon reflection I don't think they were genuine opal, and I'm not entirely sure what the mystical properties of two bits of coloured glass from an Avon catalogue actually are. I owned a lot of books with fairies painted on the cover, and most of my CDS at the time featured pre-Raphaelite paintings as album art and featured thin-voiced women singing traditional folk songs about the Corn King. And I used to wander around WP Jones and pretend I was somewhere…somewhere magical, somewhere mystical. Somewhere ancient and powerful and spiritual. Somewhere…somewhere like Dorset. Now, I'd never been to Dorset. In fact I've still never been to Dorset. I just knew Brian Froud lived in Dorset and he designed the puppets for *The Dark Crystal* and *Labyrinth* (which are blatantly the best films ever made), so I figured that Dorset was pretty damn magical. It's weird, I haven't thought about this in years.

FERGUS takes a tin box down from the mantle. It is rusty and battered. He gently places it on the gingham-covered table in front of him. FERGUS carefully lifts the lid, revealing an interior that looks like the inside of a school locker in miniature.

FERGUS: When I was at school, I knew these three girls. You
probably knew three girls just like them when you were at
school. You know, the mean girls.
For the sake of this story, we'll call them Head Cheerleader,
Homecoming Queen and
Most Likely to Succeed –
the prettiest girls you've ever seen up close
who can open and close possibilities in the vast microcosm
of high school halls
and shopping malls
draw lines
divide the haves
from the have-nots
…and all this before third period.

So anyway, one day they skip chemistry to take
Homecoming Queen's brand new SUV
to smoke a bit of weed amongst the trees
of a forest just waiting to be
a subdivision.

envision this
the unparalleled bliss of three little maids from school
made men in miniskirts
taking a break from flirting and hurting in unequal measure
to laugh
in the company of women
when
suddenly
Homecoming Queen

makes a mean right hook
connects with the head of
(you guessed it)
Head Cheerleader
and the sound of knuckle
against skull
shuts them up for a bit
'til
the silence is broken
by Most Likely to Succeed laughing
in the company of women
then a one-sided snowstorm of blows
Head Cheerleader closes her eyes
retreats inside as the bones of her nose
explode
and even with her eyes closed she knows
the world has gone red
plays dead when her friends pull her out of the car
laughing in the 'cause two's a company and three's a
crowd'
…of women
okay
so
it might have been the way Head Cheerleader
looked at rebel without a cause
plausibly the property of Homecoming Queen

that might have been the way they explained this sudden
violence away the next day
if there had been something to say
but there wasn't
shame is a great silencer

and scuffles that high in the hierarchy rarely register down
below.

So no, nothing to say.

and as her friends drive away
Head Cheerleader opens her eyes
spies the stain the mangled remains
of her nose are spewing down her shirt
and thinks
'this is my scarlet letter'

Which, to be fair, is a pretty astute observation for a girl
who never read the book
just half the CliffsNotes
(saw the movie though
it was okay
a bit gay maybe)
and see, the day the rest of us read bits aloud in class
she wasn't allowed
kept out of an over-crowded classroom
left stewing in solitary in-school detention for no better
reason
than
some teachers hate pretty girls with power

so
within the hour I'm sitting
behind the gym with Most Likely to Succeed and she's

let me in on the secret
tells me to keep it quiet
and laughs
she smokes a Kool but her hands are shaking
her voice is cool but her hands are shaking
and something is breaking apart
in her.

*FERGUS gently closes the lid of the box and hands it to you for safe
keeping. Then FERGUS pulls out a small square of paper.*

FERGUS: Do you remember the name of the street you grew
up on? Could you write it on this piece of paper?

*You do, and hand the piece of paper back. As he speaks, he begins
folding the paper, first one way and then another.*

FERGUS: Out past the football fields
(in between high school and the rest of it)
there used to be this cluster of pine trees
(felt like a forest)
Out past the football fields
(in between high school and the rest of it)
this quiet place we'd escape to
to smoke our Kools and Camel Lights
and tell each other stories.

little bits of gossip about prom queens and teenage
romances,
and saving each other's souls.

Sometimes we went there
Out past the football fields
(in between high school and the rest of it)
Sometimes we went there with the girls we went steady
with.

Asked Christie to come out with me there once.
Kissed her with my eyes screwed shut,
our knees barely touching,
green grass tickling the backs of our legs.
Kissed her with my eyes screwed shut.
(and tried not to think about her dead brother)

Kissed her with my eyes screwed shut.

Wondered once what it would be like to take David out
there sometime.
Taste David on my tongue.

Out past the football fields
(in between high school and the rest of it)
Brooke told me offhandedly that everyone was okay with
me being

the way I was, but they didn't think I should rub their faces in it.

That's Duluth for you.

(I still remember the Coca-Cola scent of her breath and the crisp virginity of her cheerleading uniform)

Out past the football fields
(in between high school and the rest of it)
I heard it's been turned into an overflow parking lot now.
Paved over
that last bit of wilderness.

FERGUS has folded the paper into an origami cicada. He adds the finished cicada to the swarm on the wall behind him. As he does, animated cicadas scurry across the window.

FERGUS: Oh, um. Sorry. I was pretty sure I'd got rid of those. Another fact about Georgia – there are bugs everywhere. I mean, everywhere.

Some more facts about Georgia

1. Atlanta has its own official Ambassador of Mirth. It's true. His name is Midtown Mary, and he is a six-foot tall Black man who dresses up in a majorette costume every day and twirls his batons up and down Peachtree Street. I swear to God, I am not making this bit up. He's been doing it for about 16 years now, and when asked he says he does it because he just wants to lift people's spirits a little, to

put a smile on their faces. Probably goes without saying, but this is a self-appointed ambassadorship and thus not recognized by any official bodies such as the UN.

2. The Brown Recluse is one of the world's most poisonous spiders, and again is indigenous to Georgia. Its bite won't kill you, but is so painful it has been described as being shot with a shotgun at close range, and the pain of it can physically knock you off your feet. The Brown Recluse likes to hide in warm, dark places like your bedclothes, or towels if you leave them on the floor, or in your shoes if you're not wearing them. Actually, its favourite place to hide is just under the lip of the rim of the toilet bowl.

3. Only Christians go to Heaven, and never drug addicts or faggots, which basically means my family is fucked.

So there's another fact about Georgia, which to be honest, I really didn't want to tell you. But up until 1998, it was still illegal to be gay in the state of Georgia. Georgia code section 16-6-2 provided a one- to twenty-year mandatory sentence for any adults consenting to 'any sexual act involving the sex organs of one person and the mouth or anus of another'. While presumably heterosexual couples were not excluded from this law, it was largely used to persecute gay people. For the purposes of comparing the severity of Georgia's opposition to these sorts of consensual acts between adults, Georgia provides less extreme penalties for sexual acts such as bestiality and necrophilia, which provide one- to five-year and one- to ten-year sentences respectively. While Georgia code section 16-6-2 was finally stuck down in 1998, similar codes existed in

states all across America. It wasn't until as recently as 2003 that the US Supreme Court finally made a ruling, which declared such codes unconstitutional under federal law.

FERGUS turns out the lights, one by one. In the window, storm clouds begin to appear. The air in the room begins to cool.

FERGUS: We waited, watched the air turn green –

The sky is smudged charcoal, the
palm trees bow deeply, genuflecting.

Earlier, the clouds were coiled, tensed, as black as
jungle cats just rising above the horizon,
rumbling.

My father is silhouetted against the strange electric sky,
a cold can of beer going warm in his hand, sweating.

We stand on the back porch, watch and wait. Silent.

When the storm comes, it sucks the light out of the air,
then

everything is plunged in violet. The air tastes like burnt
oxygen.

My mother holds us close, sings low, songs about angels
flying from Montgomery
while the world ends. Her
breath is heavy with Parliament cigarettes and Budweiser,
and I
bury myself deeper into her arms.

Afterwards, the air turns polished silver, the ground
groans under the weight of all that rain.
One of my father's friends has lost his home.
We walk from room to room, surveying the damage –
downed trees, patches of pewter sky, rain falling on the
dining room table, the
living room sofa –

I remember my father standing, silhouetted against that
sky,
and I wonder at his fearlessness. I remember the calmness
of his gaze, looking out
on all that violence
just creeping over the horizon.

*A globe next to FERGUS begins to glow softly. Instead of displaying
the countries of the world, this globe only shows a map of Georgia.*

FERGUS: You know how sometimes when you're far away
    from home –

maybe you're travelling, or maybe you've moved to a new
place – and you suddenly get this craving for something,
this certain type of food. Maybe it's something your
mother makes, or some local delicacy you can only get in
one place, and you know there's no way you can find this
food where you are, but you know if you could just have
one bite, you'd be home?

*FERGUS takes out a small glass jar of pecans. He takes out three
pecans and gently places them on the table in front of him.*

FERGUS: I was playing your Zombie Apocalypse board game
    with you.

One of your pearl back buttons had come undone.
I remember the soft seashell curl of your ear and wanting
to wrap my mouth around it, just once.

FERGUS places the first pecan in his mouth and chews slowly.

This moment tastes like a cold can of Pabst Blue Ribbon
sweating in the sun.

We went to pick her up from the house on Edgewood
Avenue. We were worried.
The front door was already open, the screen door
shuddered in the evening air, and I remember thinking
how dangerous that was in this neighbourhood.
Inside was silent, and the smell of vodka was antiseptic.

FERGUS places the second pecan in his mouth and chews slowly.

This moment tastes like Cherry Coke gone flat, viscous.

I'm four years old, and you are with me,
and the air is filled with the sound of brass and happiness.
We sit under a sycamore, a family,
The air is green and golden.

FERGUS places the third pecan in his mouth and chews slowly.

This moment tastes like warm apple pie and soft sweet
beignets.

*FERGUS takes a wooden box down from the mantle and carefully
places it on the table in from of him. He gently opens the lid and
pulls out a photo and a candle, which he lights.*

FERGUS: There's a house on a hill and

(I'm not sure I should be telling you this)
a long concrete drive snakes its way up to the door.

The house is wooden, it's a rich red brown,
like forest cake or bearskins,
The whole thing looks a little like it's made of Lincoln Logs
Maybe I'm just remembering it like that.

I used to draw bright pictures in coloured chalk along the
length of the drive,
messages to welcome my parents home.
(I'm not sure I want to tell you this)

This is the garage, and this is the patio. It runs the length of
the house.
My mother always wanted to hang baskets of flowers all
along the front.
She wanted a patio swing she could read and dream in.
She never got around to those things.

In spring, the bushes along the front would burst into lurid
pink, the front lawn would glow green, but the house on
the hill would sit back, cool and quiet in the pine tree's
shadows.
(I'm not sure)
(I don't think)
(No)

Sixteen years later I tried to find the house on the hill, but it wasn't where I remembered it. Instead, there was a flat green field, the welcome sign for a subdivision.

FERGUS blows out the candle. He places the candle and photo back inside the box. FERGUS gently closes the lid of the box and hands it to you for safekeeping.

FERGUS: I need a drink. Does anyone else need a drink? Because the bar is now open!

A neon bar light flashes on and blues music begins to play. FERGUS takes out a bottle of Southern Comfort and pours you a drink. In the window, shadowy silhouettes dance seductively.

FERGUS: Come on down to Cabbagetown!
    to 97 Estoria!
    It's the hottest bar on a hot summer day and
    the hipsters are smouldering

    it's the heat that hits you first
    Your skin slickens in
    the midday sun
    and Southern Girls don't sweat,
    they glisten.
    (that bit is true)

Come on down to Cabbagetown!

the hipsters are peacocking for anyone
who'll watch them.
These boys and girls do redneck sexy
These boys and girls do redneck cool.

Look at JennyLynne sitting at the bar
liquid eyeliner and the best night of your life,
Southern belle and hellfire.

Look at Old Johnny-boy
dreaming about Sundays
plays Woodie Guthry on the Jukebox
and thinks himself political

Come on down to Cabbagetown!
It's hot as sin and skin is on display
skin spidered with tattoos
bright and bold in the hazy heat
ink glowing
like stained glass windows
a space to save your soul

In Cabbagetown on an August afternoon
Mosquitoes suck and hum
and the air thrums with sex
and danger.

The blues music fades away.

Clink clink
goes the tinkling melody of ice in a glass
and a hand clasped around its contents

(the diluted mocha, ochre and smokey colour of the
measures of whiskey – takes ten years to make it that way
and ten minutes to drink it)

The glass in his hand sweats softly in the swampland sun
but
he doesn't.

he's as cool as a copperhead snake
baking its honey coloured scales in the sun and
sipping the afternoon air with a forked tongue

He's as cool as an alligator grin
Swimming deep in murky water with a belly full of
innocent things
He's as mean as a wildcat in heat.

keeps you just on the cusp of cuming
sweating and shaking with a look that could break bones in
his eyes.

has a voice like a summer storm
warm

American Alligator

(*Crocodilus mississipiensis*)

sweaty

sticky

*FERGUS takes another box down from the mantle. It is dirty and
scratched. He gently places it on the gingham-covered table in front
of him. FERGUS carefully lifts the lid, revealing rusty nails.*

FERGUS: On 21 February 1997, a pipe bomb exploded at the
Otherside Lounge, a popular gay nightclub in Atlanta, GA.

The bomb had been planted in the bar by Eric Rudolph,
who between 1996 and 1998, committed a number of
bombings which killed two people and injured at least 150
others in the name of an anti-abortion and anti-gay agenda.

One of the most seriously injured of the patrons at the
Otherside Lounge that night underwent surgery to remove
a three to four inch nail from her arm, which had severed
a brachial artery. She was at the Otherside that evening to
celebrate a friend's birthday.

Prior to the bombing, she had only told a few people that
she was a lesbian. However, she was 'outed' when the
media reported that she had been among the causalities.
As a result, she was fired from her job at a real estate
agency.

FERGUS gently closes the lid of the box and hands it to you for safekeeping.

FERGUS takes another box down from the mantle. He gently places it on the gingham-covered table in front of him.

FERGUS: I have a present for you.

FERGUS carefully lifts the lid, revealing ripe peaches. He offers you a peach and invites you to eat it. In the window, a train can be seen passing under a star-filled sky.

FERGUS: It's closing time at Trackside Tavern and

Ol' Nick is still nursing his drink. The Pabst Blue Ribbon gone warm in his hand and he's ready to fight the world.

It's closing time at Trackside Tavern and
Johnny-boy does the dishes and wishes it was Sunday.
Johnny-boy does the dishes and wishes
he was young again.
Johnny-boy wonders what happened to his best friend
the one he kissed one time
the one who tasted like
homecoming.

It's closing time at Trackside Tavern and

Christian is telling that same story again.

It's closing time at Trackside Tavern and Ol' Nick is going.
Knows when he's not wanted.
Neon lights flash and blind his eyes as
he pitch and tumbles out into
the warm night air of Dekalb Avenue.
The line of the highway stretches out in both directions.
He can't remember which one takes him home

Remembers his Chevy out back, hesitates and waits for a
cab instead.
None coming, and the August air is sticky and sweet
with Southern Comfort.

His mind is sticky and sweet
with Southern Comfort.

He's stuck for a second,
a bluebottle stunned and hovering by
the blue light of a bug zapper

and suddenly, a star appears.
A purpose.

See, Ol' Nick loves a girl named Darla, a bartender
on the other side of town.

Darla's got a voice thick with whiskey and gravel,
and when she asked you what you're havin'
most boys forget their beer orders.
Darla's the innuendo of her hips, the sticky patch of her
back
where her blouse sticks in the midday sun.
Makes you think fresh peaches and sticky fingers.

Everyone's in love with Darla the bartender, and
Ol' Nick loves her completely.
Sang Wanda Jackson when her back was turned,
left her a copy of Jack Black's *You Can't Win* instead of a tip
and dreamed of her and Coney Island.

Now Ol' Nick knows where he's going, the hope of her
making his legs work again.

And off he stumbles, mumbling poetry under his beer
breath.
He's a man with a mission and
the vision of her will be
enough to make the world stop spinning.

(listen to the sound of the train whistle in the distance, the
chug and syncopation of the train making its way towards
us, sings low, don't know if it's going or coming)

Ol' Nick hears this, thinks briefly, something about

the shortest distance and
the point of all this.
It'll be easier to follow the twin lines of the train tracks,
tracks'll take him through Decatur
out past East Atlanta
Something like a stairway to heaven.

He's hoping for the straightest line between him
and his heart's desire.
However, half of the highway patrol in the greater Atlanta
area could tell you that on a night like this Ol' Nick
might find straight line walking well nigh impossible.

Tonight he pitch and tumbles along the tracks, slack-jawed
and hoping.
He's a man with a mission.
sticky fingers and fresh peaches

Needs a piss.   .

Needs a rest.

Needs his head to stop sounding like the inside of an
ocean.

Has a piss.

Needs a rest.

Forgets where he is for a second.

Fresh peaches. Sticky fingers.

Can't remember if he's dreaming.

Ol' Nick finally comes to rest
in the bed the train trestles make,
and his heart aches for her, Darla the bartender.

He pretends he's already in her arms
he can taste the bit of her back where her shirt sticks.

Sticky fingers.

Sleep settles into him,
the whistle doesn't wake him.
Sounds like a love song, the chug and syncopation
of the train making its way towards him is
the distant beat of her heart, not his own tragic ending.

Fresh peaches.

FERGUS takes another box down from the mantle. It is covered with bits of broken mirror. He gently places it on the gingham-covered table in front of him. FERGUS carefully lifts the lid, revealing black feathers. He takes out the feathers, raises them above his head, and as he speaks lets them slowly spin to the floor one by one.

FERGUS: Crow is crying at the heavens again
  She's trying to sing down the sun.
  Another man has done and left her.
  (and the hurt of it burns like Atlanta)
  She's wilted hibiscus, bruised jasmine
  She's a flower bed going to seed
  (and a drag queen weeping on Peachtree Street is the saddest thing).
  I'll fly away, she thinks,
  finish this cigarette and fly away.

.

FERGUS takes another box down from the mantle. It is silver and shiny. He gently places it on the gingham-covered table in front of him. FERGUS carefully lifts the lid, revealing a tiny mirrored disco ball sparkling in neon light.

Midtown Mary whistles by
He's a one man Pride parade
Gaiety and mirth
Black asphalt Atlanta cracks a smile
He's teaching Atlanta to laugh
and as he passes redknecks rubberneck left and right
The light shining off his silver batons is blinding, dazzles them.

I'll fly away, thinks Crow.
I'm flying, think Mary
(listen to the whistle of a train going by)

FERGUS gently closes the lid of both boxes and hands them to you for safekeeping.

FERGUS pulls away the gingham tablecloth, revealing a battered wooden crate underneath. As he speaks, he collects each of the boxes back from you and places them gently in the crate.

FERGUS: These things are at least almost always at least
    halfway true.

In Georgia, all dusty red roads lead home –
the bones of my father are buried there
Midtown Mary twitches his tranny ass
Majorettes his way from
Auburn Street to North Avenue
Sequins and tassles and
no one ever hassles her,
not once –

No, that's not quite it

In Georgia, we've all got
smiles as crooked and wise as pecan pies and

hearts as soft as doughy white biscuits.
We listen
and languish under fans on verandas
Our eyes are as cool as air-conditioning.

No, that's not quite it

In Atlanta, in evening
the streets are paved with gold, the
sky turns molten
and the golden dome of the capital building looks
like the spires of Heaven.

That's true.
That bit's true.

FERGUS removes a final box from the mantle. It is wooden and unassuming. He gently places it in front of his heart. As he speaks, he slowly pulls back one side of the box to reveal a tiny Atlanta skyline bathed in blue light.

You probably can't find my Georgia
You probably can't find it.
But if you rest your head in the small of my chest
you'll feel the August heat against your cheek
and the cicadas are singing.

This is almost always at least halfway true.

This is true.

FERGUS gently places the final box in the crate with all of the others, smiles at you, and walks out the door.

The End